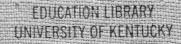

SARAH JOSEPHA HALE

Mary Had a Little Lamb

pictures by Salley Mavor

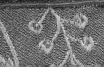

ORCHARD BOOKS NEW YORK

Mary had a little lamb,

little lamb, little lamb,

Mary had a little lamb,

its fleece was white as snow.

And everywhere that Mary went,

Mary went, Mary went,

And everywhere that Mary went,

the lamb was sure to go.

It followed her to school one day,

school one day, school one day,

It followed her to school one day,

which was against the rule.

It made the children laugh and play,

laugh and play, laugh and play,

It made the children laugh and play

to see a lamb at school.

And so the teacher turned it out,

turned it out, turned it out,

And so the teacher turned it out,
but still it lingered near,

And waited patiently about
till Mary did appear.

"What makes the lamb love Mary so?"
the eager children cry;

"Oh, Mary loves the lamb, you know,"
the teacher did reply.

While Sarah Josepha Hale is known and credited as the author of "Mary Had a Little Lamb," there is some debate about the authorship of the first twelve lines. Mary Elizabeth Sawyer of Sterling, Massachusetts, who claimed to be the original "Mary" of the poem, said she rescued a newborn lamb forsaken by its mother and nursed it back to life with catnip tea. The lamb became her pet, followed her everywhere, and they became fast friends. Having few neighbors or dolls to play with, she even dressed the lamb in pantalets. One day, in 1813, the lamb started following Mary to school. Her brother Nat suggested they take the lamb with them. The rest, according to Mary Elizabeth Sawyer, happened just as the poem tells it, for a young man named John Roulstone was visiting the school that day and was so taken with the incident of the lamb that he returned the next day, handing Mary a slip of paper with the first twelve lines of the poem as we know it today.

Some believe Sarah Josepha Hale wrote the entire poem; others believe that she added additional verses to those that appear here. While the debate over the authorship is unresolved, the poem itself, whatever version is read or recited, has captured the imagination of children ever since it was first published in 1830.

The original poem, as Mary Elizabeth Sawyer said she received it from John Roulstone:

> Mary had a little lamb;
>   Its fleece was white as snow;
> And everywhere that Mary went,
>   the lamb was sure to go.
>
> It followed her to school one day,
>   Which was against the rule;
> It made the children laugh and play
>   To see the lamb at school.
>
> And so the teacher turned it out;
>   But still it lingered near,
> And waited patiently about
>   Till Mary did appear.

The artwork for this book is fabric relief. This art form includes many techniques, including appliqué, embroidery, wrapping, dyeing, and soft sculpture. The background fabrics were dyed and then sewn together. Three-dimensional pieces were made from a variety of materials, including covered and stuffed cardboard shapes, wrapped wire, found objects such as beach stones and driftwood, and fabric. The lamb's fleece was made of french knots, using fine wool yarn. Details were embroidered onto the shapes and background, and then the three-dimensional pieces were sewn into place. All stitching was done by hand.

Color transparencies of the artwork were made by Thomas N. Kleindinst and reproduced in full color. The text of the book was set in 30 point Adobe Goudy. The book was printed by Barton Press, Inc., and bound by Horowitz/Rae.

To my parents — S. M.

Illustrations copyright © 1995 by Salley Mavor

Orchard Books, 95 Madison Avenue, New York, NY 10016

Manufactured in the United States of America
Printed by Barton Press, Inc. Bound by Horowitz/Rae. Book design by Susan M. Sherman

10 9 8 7 6 5 4 3 2 1

Library of Congress Cataloging-in-Publication Data
Hale, Sarah Josepha Buell, 1788-1879.
   Mary had a little lamb / by Sarah Josepha Hale ; pictures by Salley Mavor.
   p. cm.
   "A Melanie Kroupa Book."
   Summary: Fabric relief illustrations accompany this familiar nursery rhyme about a young girl whose lamb follows her to school. Includes information about the history of the rhyme.
   ISBN 0-531-06875-7. — ISBN 0-531-08725-5 (lib. bdg.)
   1. Lambs — Juvenile poetry. 2. Nursery rhymes, American. 3. Children's Poetry, American. [1. Nursery rhymes. 2. American poetry.] I. Mavor, Salley, ill. II. Title.
PS1774.H2M3   1995
811' .2 — dc20   94-24847

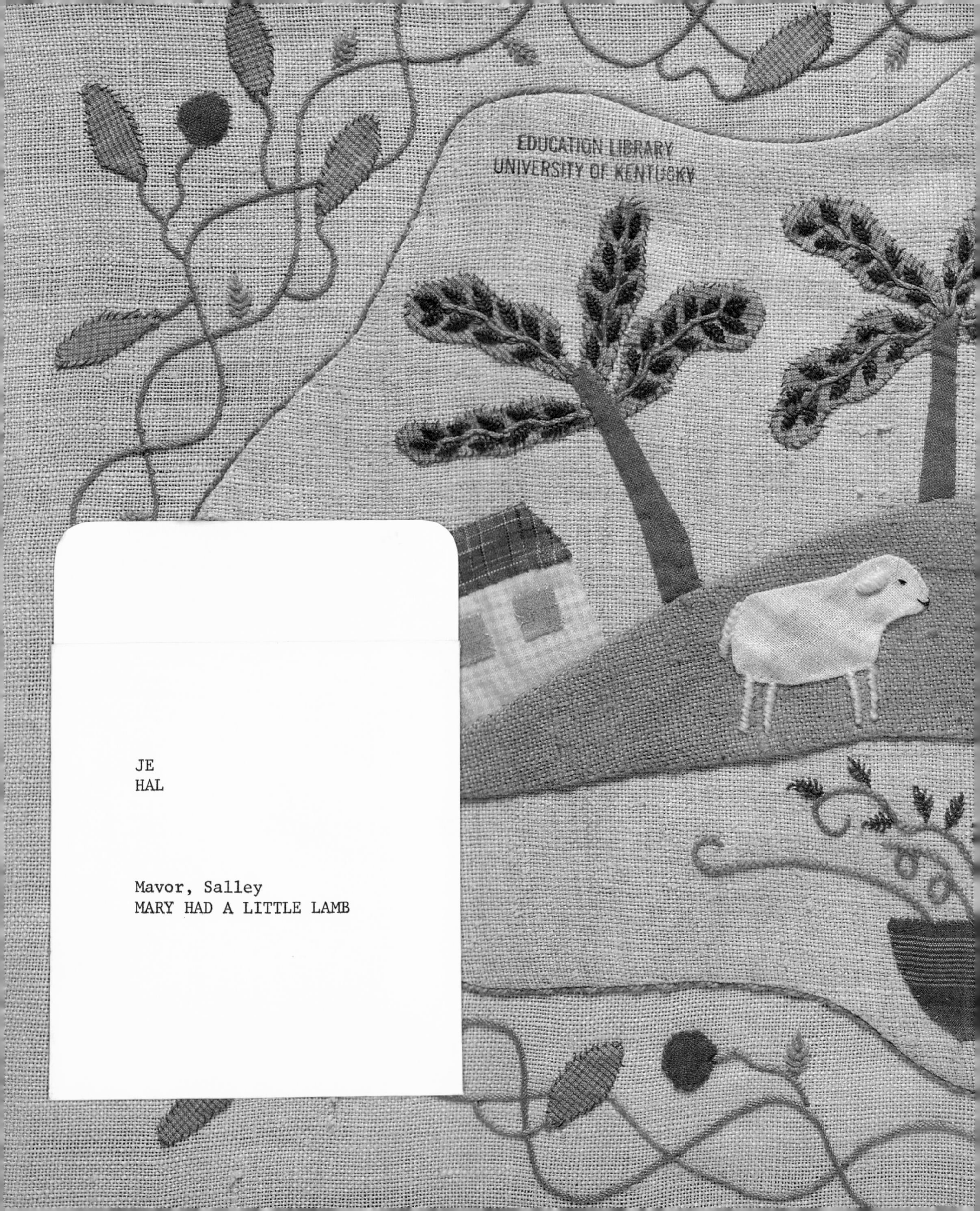